A Month of Mondays

Poems and Prayers for the Monday
Morning Homemaker Blues

Mary Lou Carney

ABINGDON PRESS   NASHVILLE

A MONTH OF MONDAYS:

POEMS AND PRAYERS
FOR THE MONDAY MORNING HOMEMAKER BLUES

Copyright © 1984 by Abingdon Press

Library of Congress Cataloging in Publication Data

Carney, Mary Lou, 1949-
    A month of Mondays.
    1. Housewives—Prayer-books and devotions—English.
I. Title.
BV4844.C327   1984   242'.6435   84-2823

ISBN 0-687-27164-9

MANUFACTURED BY THE PARTHENON PRESS AT
NASHVILLE, TENNESSEE, UNITED STATES OF AMERICA

for my husband
Gary

who helps me through
Mondays
and other traumas

Spring

1

Rain.

A cold spring rain
  thuds against my kitchen window.

Drops race to the bottom of the pane,
  disappearing in the fat white line
    of chalky caulking.

I hate rainy Mondays, God.

I pick up the green plastic sprinkling can,
  begin the methodical watering of
    parched house plants.

Water falls in unsteady streams,
  hitting the trunk of my weeping fig
  making mud puddles in ebony potting soil.

A splash of color catches my eye.

I reach behind the parlor palm for
  my Christmas cactus—
stuck there months ago when its
  water-spotted leaves
gave little hope of flowers.

Now,
  plush crimson blossoms weight the leaves;
  folded buds promise even more beauty.

I place this piece of Christmas
  in my kitchen window,
where it stands resplendent
  against a watery April Monday.

And my heart is stirred
  with the possibilities of patience

for people
  as well as plants.

2

It's Monday, God.
  Again.

And as I stand here in the shower
  letting the water splat against my forehead
my mind buzzes with
  unfinished weekend projects
  unfound Sunday leisure
    an avalanche of Monday morning drudgeries.

I don't feel refreshed, Lord—
  or eager
  or even capable of
    meeting what this week holds.

So take my hand;
  lead me gently through the routine of today.
Open my eyes—
  spiritually and literally

because

it's Monday, God.
  Again.

3

Monday morning gloom
  hangs thick around me—
    as tangible as
      scattered Sunday papers.

I wade through remnants
  of weekend revelry:
    Legos
    doll clothes
    sports editions
    cap-gun ammunition.

Fisher-Price people
  sprawl beneath the table,
    round bodies half-buried
    in worn shag carpet.

So much to do!

I carry dirty dishes to the kitchen,
  balancing milk-ringed glasses
    bowls with stray, buttery kernels.

I grab at a nearby pile,
  find my daughter's piano piece
    protruding from beneath
      abandoned Sunday school papers.

"Sonatina: For Piano Solo"

Inside,
  proud eighth notes
  agile sixteenths
    splash the page with
      splatterings of black.

I remember when
    first she saw the music—
her wide-eyed cry of
    "I'll never be able to play all this!"

But measure by measure
        line by line
            page by page
        melodies emerged.
Fingers stumbled—
    then flew—
over ivory keys.

Measure by measure . . .

I glance around the cluttered room.

Papers first—
    then toys.
Dishes and dusting last.
A load of clothes
    while I bake bazaar cupcakes.

Measure by measure

I find myself
    humming an old dance tune

and

feeling the dissipation of
    Monday morning gloom.

4

On this Monday morning—
   with the heady scent of lilacs
      filling the air,

I begin my spring cleaning.

The hall closet is first—
   where piles of ill-folded blankets
      mountains of lumpy pillows
plummet onto the floor
   each time the door is opened.

I pull snatches
      of satin trim,
   make piles of like colors
      for trips to the washer.

Then from a back corner,
      it tumbles down on me—

my grandmother's quilt.

I finger the fine stitches,
   remembering Grandma's gnarled knuckles
      big-eyed needles.

I recognize the pieces:
   lavender of an Easter dress long-forgotten
   red print from my sister's favorite blouse
   a patch of blue flowers formerly a pocket
      on Mother's apron.

I bury my face in the quilt.

It smells faintly of
   dust
      soap
         cedar.

And I remember countless cold nights
    when Grandma layered me
      in colorful warmth.

I carry the quilt
    to the line,
squinting into springtime sun
    as I clothespin yellowing corners.

And while I watch breezes blow
    these bits of colored cloth,
I realize how much my life
    is like this quilt—

patterned with
    dark patches
    bright splashes

stitched together with
    God's patience
      persistence
        love.

5

Slippered feet scuff across
  faded linoleum floors.
The sound of soap opera dialogue
  drifts through the dayroom door.
Someone is playing "Chopsticks"
  on the battered piano down the hall.

Aunt Ida sits in her room—
  propped in a big orange chair,
    staring at a curtain-shrouded window.

Above her bed hangs a huge calendar,
  courtesy of OLSEN'S FUNERAL HOME.
Its black numbers perch in sallow squares
  like impatient vultures.

Her mouth doesn't close quite right;
  spit dangles from the edge of her lip
    drops silently onto her huge bib.

She seems unaware of me,
  as I open her window
    place a potted geranium on its sill.

I talk of spring and Holland tulips
  the children and summer plans
  committee work and needlepoint
    and broccoli soup.

She could be a statue,
      a personification of old age
      captured in wax
except for that thin line of spit,
  as fine as the sugar threads she used to spin
    making Christmas candy.

I hurry into the sunshine,
   feeling—as I squint—
the deepening wrinkles
   around my own eyes.

Old age scares me, God—
   makes me want to cling to youth
   with a clawing, clutching grip.

Show me, Lord
   the blessings of long life—
the lull in the daily bustle
   that will allow for more
      time spent with you.

Remind me that
   service is not a stack of church committee work
                  a state of scurry and flutter
but rather a commitment of the heart.

for some of the greatest
   prayer warriors of all
      serve from rocking chairs.

So grant me, oh God,
   the courage to
      grow old gracefully—

secure in the knowledge
   that he who held my hand
through the sunshine of childhood
      wonder of adolescence
         demands of adulthood

will not leave me
   at four-score and three.

6

Green snatches of
   shredded cellophane grass
lie in sparse patches
   on my family room rug.

Baskets now boasting only
   jellybeans and candy wrappers
sit dejectedly atop my
   finger-smudged coffee table.

A decapitated chocolate bunny
   lies melting in
      reluctant April sun.

Somehow the color and pageantry of Easter
   seem so much further away
      than only yesterday.

As I reach for the melting mess,
   a mass of lavender
      rolls from behind the drape—
a forgotten Easter egg.

Its shell is finely cracked;
   tiny lines crisscross its surface
      like winding roads on a pastel map.

This one egg
   eluded the children
in the frenzied flurry
   of hiding and finding.

I stand over the kitchen sink
      to peel my purple egg,
         watch shattered shell fall away

to reveal a flawless surface
of pearly white.

I place it on a plate and,
armed with salt and pepper,
prepare to make a meal
of this egg-hunt fugitive.

But first I bow my head
to offer thanks for
lost things found,
inner beauty,

and for this
battered bit of Easter
come to color my Monday
with just a touch of wonder.

7

Fly specks as old
as last summer's memories
   stubbornly stay on my windows.

I spray on more cleaner,
   watch turquoise rivulets
      run down the panes.

My rag squeaks across the glass
   as my thumbnail pushes
      at each imperfection.

In a flurry of
   ammonia and industry
the fly specks disappear.

Sunlight streams through the window,
   touching the chandelier.
A thousand tiny tendrils of light
   radiate from its prisms.

My own image
   looks out at me
      from the streakless glass.

I push a stray strand
   back under my bandanna
      and wonder . . .

How well can God
   reflect his love
      through me?

What specks of selfishness
      or apathy
   cloud the window of my soul?

"Wash me, O Lord,
   and I shall be clean."

The words replay in my head,
   a tidbit of truth
      salvaged from some forgotten sermon.

I move on to other windows
   scrub with new vigor
      pray with each swipe of my cloth,
         "Wash *me,* O Lord" . . .

determined that this spring
   all my windows will be clean—
      inside
         and
            out.

8

This weekend
  my daughter went to her first
slumber party—
  an all-night affair
featuring
  pizza and
    popcorn and
      giggling.

There are other firsts, too—
  like washing her own hair,
    bathing without a struggle,
      trading her Under-Roos
        for a training bra.

And always before, at bedtime—
  when hugs and prayers were through—
she met my bent-over kiss with,
  "Please leave on a light."

But last night's final comment,
  spoken in a voice I hardly knew,
was, "Tomorrow morning please make sure
  the curling iron is hot."

Dear God
  it seems these changes
    are coming on too fast.
  Childhood is a special time—
    I want to make it last.

Help me, Father.
  Grant me wisdom.

Let me not be

a mother who clings
to her offspring.

Teach me the truth
  of these changing things:

the caterpillar doesn't die—
  the butterfly takes wing!

9

Smudged snowdrifts
  cower beside
    t
      h
        a
          w
          i
            n
              g
roadways.

Fat-breasted robins
  play tug-of-war with
  rubbery, wriggly worms.

A courageous crocus
  pokes its head through ground
  still cold from February frost.

This March Monday,
  all nature seems to vibrate
with the imminence of
  SPRING!

I walk around the yard,
  check my almond bush for buds
    my roses for winter kill

when suddenly I see it,
  glistening in the colorless grass:

the first dandelion.

"Not already!"
  I groan.

Defiantly,
  I pluck it.

But as I hold it under my chin,
  I smile to remember
    days of endless sunshine
    childish chants of
      "You like butter"
    fragile chains of fuzzy blossoms.

I run my finger
  across the flower;
it feels like
  kitten fur.

Impulsively,
  I stick this unlikely boutonniere
  through a button hole in my blouse.

After all,
  it's spring!

And I can hardly wait
    for baseball
      barbecues
  and dandelion bouquets.

10

Yesterday was Mother's Day—

but no stained-glass sermons
   four-color cards
      stem-dyed carnations
   filled my holiday.

Instead,
   the day was spent
      with my seven-year-old
         at a state wrestling meet.

I look down from
   high, hard bleachers
on faded purple padding.

Wrestlers tease and touch each other,
            trip and tangle guys twice their weights
      till colorful singlets
         lie fluttering on the mat
            like parade confetti.

Coaches with serious eyes
   corral their young athletes,
who alternate between
   practicing pins
      playing tag.

The matches begin,
   weighting the air with
      dull thuds
         muffled grunts.

Legs and arms entwine
   as bodies roll across mats,

opponents looking like awkward tortoises
    locked in mortal combat.

Referees flatten their cheeks to the floor,
    strain to see
        if a pin is really a pin
    or just a close call
for the back-arching boy on the bottom.

So my Mother's Day passes—

filled with the sound of whistle shrills
                the taste of warm Gatorade
suffused with the smells of fresh popcorn
                        old knee pads
consummated by my own son's
    snaggletoothed grin
        of triumph.

Then this morning,
    when I went to make beds,
lumpy covers were smoothed over his pillow
    and folded there was a piece of
        rough-torn, wide-lined paper.
On it were these words:
    TO THE BEST MOM I HAVE HAD EVER

Now, as I stuff his
    singlet and sweatshirt
        into the dirty clothes,

I smile at the memory of
    yesterday's moments shared
        with my son

and realize
    it just may have been
        the best Mother's Day
            I have had
ever.

11

Monday morning
  aerobics—

The instructor flashes a
  flawless smile at our
    sleepy eyes
    sagging bellies.

"Okay, girls!
Let's wake up those muscles!"

Her trim hips
    lithe limbs,
  outlined by black leotards,
bend and twist
  in effortless rhythm.

She looks like
  a whip of licorice
    with perfect timing.

I feel muscles tighten;
  a traveling tingle
    threatens a cramp.

"Come on, girls!
Just fifteen more sit-ups to go!"

Familiar pain
  clutches my gut
    with clawing fingers.

I keep thinking of
  warm Danish
  coffee with double cream.

And the bakery
　　is right on my way home.

Help me, God.

Remind me that
　　my body is your creation
　　　　your temple.

Keep me from the
　　beckoning paths of
　　　　gluttony
　　　　　　indolence
　　　　　　　　apathy.

Encourage me
　　as I grit my teeth
　　　　grind my way
through

Monday morning
　　aerobics.

12

This Memorial Day morning
  finds me walking through
    graveyard grass.
Each blade is heavy
  and wet with dew,
as though Night has wept out
  some silent grief.

Crabgrass and dandelions
  sprout from the graves of
    dark-clad ministers
    childless spinsters.
My father's grave
  is graced by rounded turf.
I touch the granite headstone—
  it is rough, hard, cold.

I close my eyes and am a child again,
  feeling the coolness
    of flat, gray creek rocks
  worn smooth by
    my bare, brown feet.

I pick a daisy
  nodding near the bank.
    "He loves me.
    He loves me not."
He seldom ever loves me.

I fling crushed petals into the creek,
  watching ripples carry them
past snags of snake dens
  and bank-fed grasses.

I load my arms with
   black-eyed Susans,
   daisies, dandelions
that grow among the alfalfa
   like crisscrossing veins of gold.

I turn to see
   my father mending fence.
With eyes the color of smoky marble
   he glares at me through
     barbed wire squares.
"There's chores to be done, young'un.
Reckon your tomfoolery can wait."

I run toward the house,
   strewing the dusty path
with trailing splashes of
   white, yellow, black.

I open my eyes.

Tiny flags flutter
   on the graves of veterans;
the smell of peonies
   perfumes the air.
I watch as Sun
   spreads itself across the graves,
drying Night's tears
   tempting open the eyelids of irises.

I am in no hurry,

for today I will give my father
   the things I could never
     give him before—

   my time
   my love
and a freshly picked daisy bouquet.

13

Sirens crash against
   Monday morning stillness.
Trucks with flashing lights
   wink like giant Cyclopes
   in the predawn darkness.

I lift the shade and see the flames,
   clutching for the sky
   with hot, orange fingers.

The old Montoney house,
   for years a haunt of
      curious school children
      imaginary ghouls
burns garishly,
   its stoic demise
undaunted by rubber-robed firemen
         arcs of endless water.

I watch as fire
   licks its way
      around window frames.

Timbers scream.

Finally,
   with audible groans,
      rafters give way.

A hundred thousand memories
   crash into smoldering rubble,
while windborne ashes
   fall on fences and porch roofs
      like sooty snow.

And I remember
   Christmas caroling—
standing clustered on the wide round porch
singing "Silent Night" through frosty puffs of white
   till Mrs. Montoney brought out
      platters of her homemade
      peanut butter fudge.

Thank you, Father
   for the miracle of memories—
those treasured recollections
   tucked away inside my heart
that spring, surprisingly, to life
   like roadside daffodils.

Through the glare of my own window
   I shiver now to see
ghostly smoke hover
   over the old house—

perhaps pausing,
   as am I,
to relish one last memory
   before daylight
      debris
         reality.

Summer

14

This first Monday of summer
 neighborhood garage sale signs
pop from lawns like June petunias.

Tacked to light poles, street signs,
 Laundromat bulletin boards;
Made of cardboard, plywood,
 pages ripped from scribble pads.

These kindred Magic-Marker signs
 shout at each passer-by:

 YARD SALE!
 RUMMAGE SALE!!
SIX-FAMILY SPECTACULAR!

Freshly patched drives
 are dotted with makeshift tables,
 bowed with the weight of
 Pablum-stained T-shirts
 paintless metal tops
 rows of read and reread romances.

Newly ironed old clothes
 fill backyard clotheslines,
their faded styles drooping
 onto wire hangers.

Such an assortment of junk—
 and jewels
 of trash—
 and treasure.

For rummaging through
 such stacks and piles
I have been known to find

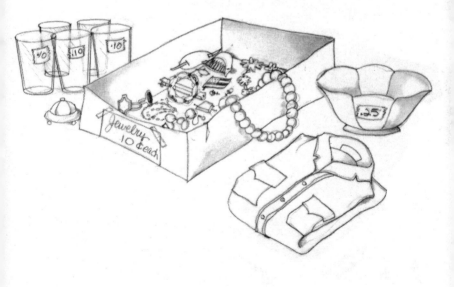

a name-dropper top for my daughter
  a good-as-new Matchbox garage
    a blouse that just matches my new blue skirt.

Later,
as I drive home—
  brown bags bulging
    beside me—
I smile at my diligence
  in digging out these bargains

and waiting for the corner light,
  pray a sudden prayer
to use my
  time and tenacity

not only in finding
  the best
    in my neighbors' garage sales
but also in finding
  the best
    in my neighbors themselves.

15

We drive through
  sifted-sunlight mornings,
    air heavy with the promise of heat,
on our way to Vacation Bible School.

My son sits beside me,
  mouthing the words of his memory verse
  wrinkling his nose each time he
    stumbles over "II Corinthians."

"I'll never get it!"
  he pouts,
    his bottom lip protruding
    like a Ubangi tribesman's.
"And I really want
  one of those neat
    blue ribbons."

I listen while he reads repeatedly
  the words of his daily verse,
his desperation deepening
  as each intersection
    brings us closer to the church.

So I remind him
  of yesterday afternoon
    when that soccer game seemed so important
  of last evening
    when he just had to watch T.V.

"I know, Mom,"
  he wails.
"But I didn't *need* this Bible verse
  till today!"

I wince with the
   familiarity
of his reasoning,
recalling how often
   I postpone
      Bible reading
      scripture study
      time alone with God

until I need,
   desperately need,
consolation
   peace
      help.

I watch my son as he walks toward the church,
   crumpled memory verse fluttering
      from his fist
   scuffed toes stubbing
      loose gravel.

He disappears into the
   jostling group of children,

while I pray for
   wisdom to teach him
the fine art of finding time
   for *all* truly important things,

realizing with chagrin
   that this is a lesson
I haven't
   quite
      learned
myself.

16

Mt. Baldy's
  146 feet of shifting sand
towers above me.

Other more adventurous tourists
  already scramble up the face
    of this fearsome sand dune.

I stand at the bottom,
  kicking clumps of beach grass
  ignoring shouts from my family
    urging me to try.

The sun is an ivory circle
  surrounded by rings of orange.
Sand blows against my legs,
  sticks to my perspiring palms.

I begin the climb.

For every three steps forward
  I slide back two.

My leg muscles throb;
  hair lies on my forehead
  in sweaty strands.

My husband,
  whose strong form
    seems easily to mount
      the mountain of sand
calls back:
  "It's easier if you walk
    in someone's footprints!"

I find the imprint
    of his ridged running shoe,
  plant my feet firmly,
      stretching my stride
        to match the meandering tracks.

He is right!

Gasping
  but exhilarated
I stand atop
  Mt. Baldy—
watching spatterings of sailboats
  floating on a surface of endless blue
feeling cool lake breezes
  caress my flushed cheeks.

And now on this Monday morning,
  as I shake sand from
    blue jean cuffs
    tennis shoes

remind me, Lord
  of the importance of struggle
    the beauty of mountain tops.

In the midst
  of this mundane Monday
let me pause, God
  to find
    and follow
your footprints.

17

Tall grass stretches before me,
  shimmering in oppressive
    August heat.
I shove my lawn tractor
  into high gear,
watching bits of green
  spew from under the deck.

Suddenly
  the air is pierced
    with shrill cries of a killdeer.
The bird circles above me,
  swooping close to my face
  battering my mower with her wings.

I swerve toward the middle of the yard.

She disappears into
  a clump of uncut grass.
Abandoning my machine,
  I stealthily approach the spot.

There, amid the camouflaging green,
  is her nest—
small, neat,
  filled with spotted treasure.

I finish my mowing—
  giving wide berth
    to that special clump of grass
  thinking of unborn birds
    cuddled beneath downy wings
and
  pondering the eternal wonder
    of the Father's own
      love for me.

18

Its giant carcass floats
  on murky Lake Michigan water.
Squeals and screams pierce summer air
  as my swimmers scramble from the
lifeless touch of
  this monster coho.
No warm water beauty this one—
  with flesh the color of Crisco,
    a gaping hole in its side the scene of
    some carrion-eater's unfinished feast.

With maternal audacity,
  I wade in waist-deep.

Small awed eyes
  watch from a safe distance
    my attempts to beach
      this deceased fish.
With a sun-bleached limb
  I struggle to pull him ashore—
fighting the will of currents
  feeling the smack of dank waves against my cheeks
    thrilling to eager cheers urging my success.

In a shallow grave
  the coho now lies,
with speckled sand
  grating his staring eyes—
with laughing children
  throwing sticks on the mound
    of muddy sand

while I sit a bit taller,
  thankful for the chance to be
    my children's hero—
if only for this afternoon.

19

All morning long I've
  paced the perimeters of my life—
from dirty diapers
  to unmade beds
from crusty oven
  to sprouting crabgrass.

Round every corner
  lurks an irksome
    "what if————?"
to tantalize and tease
  to taunt me about
    past choices
      decisions
        opportunities.

Help me today, God
  for my life seems
    painfully
      ordinary.

Defend me, Father, from the
  terror of the "ifs."
Keep me from playing the
  game of "what-might-have-been."

Remind me that true success
  is not measured by
    records broken
    mountains conquered
    minks and Mercedes acquired

but rather
  by finding
and doing
  your will—

which just may be
today for me
to make my way through
diapers and
crabgrass and
"ifs."

20

The pool quivers with the kicking
  of three dozen pairs of feet.
Bare arms flail and splash
  against the wet wonder
    beneath, around, and
      (g
       l
        u
         b
         !)
  above them.

On brown metal bleachers
  we parents sit,
    in air that is thick and cottony.

I study the instructor—
her legs are long and tan;
  stray wisps of hair
    escape from her ponytail.
Her voice is quiet
        firm
         patient.

Every eye watches
  as she skims through chlorinated water:
    backstroke, flutter kick, prone float.

Each child studies her moves,
  awed by this wonder-person who
    flaunts diving-board feats
    braves twelve-foot depths.

One
　by
one
　　she coaches them
　　　　　into the deep end
　　　　promises them
　　　　　she'll stay close.

Sweat forms on my upper lip
　as I strain to see
　　tiny faces reappear above
water that looks like turquoise Jell-O.

Remind me, Lord
that when
　I
"pass through the waters"
　you
are there.

Teach me
　to trust you
completely—

even
　when I can't
　　touch bottom.

21

In the humid heat of late July
   I thump thick green melons—
      trying to find just the one
      for our family picnic.

My eyes drift to an ill-kept corner
   where unbought marigolds and petunias
   languish in tiny plastic trays.

I think of my own annuals—
   secure and lush
      in the rich black earth
      of my flower garden.

I glance again at the cluttered corner.
   Poor unbought things!

And standing there,
   in the midst of melons and fruit flies,
I smile to think that
   I need not struggle
      in the shallow soil
       of my own strength—

for I have been bought
           redeemed
            transplanted
into the fertile soil
   of God's love and care.

As I turn into my driveway
   I pause
      to look at bright colors
        surrounding my mailbox
        to thank God for marigolds—
        and miracles.

22

The front door
  slams shut,
its shattering sound
  echoing off
    hallway walls.

The air now is
  stifling and still,
heavy with memories of
    hasty insults
      heated complaints.

The whole thing replays in my head—
  like a scene from an old movie:
    overly dramatic
    badly staged.

Yet that's the way it is, God—
  more and more often.

My marriage lies on the shelf
  like a wilted daisy.
And I can't even remember
  who first forgot
    to water it—
or why.

Help us both, Lord
  not to take out
frustrations
    on each other,
  not to misdirect
anger
    to those most near.

Remind us of
   laughter shared
      better days
marriage vows.

Let us resist the urge to
   keep score.
Let us strive, instead, to
   keep love.

Be thou the core
   of our relationship, God.

For even wilted daisies
   respond to

love and
   care and
      Living Water.

23

The tiny table top
  lies buried beneath
    boxes of tissue
    bottles of aspirin
              antibiotics
          vitamin C.

A sticky tablespoon
  lies beside an empty brown bottle
    of cough syrup.

My head throbs
  like a smashed finger.

I breathe through my mouth,
  labored
    loud—
like the soundtrack
  of a late-night horror flick.

I am so tired, God—
  for days I've been fighting this cold,
    fighting and losing.

I am sick of being sick
        of taking—religiously—
            sour, chalky remedies.

I just want to burrow under the covers,
  disappear into their security
    the way I used to
      sink into my grandma's
        feather bed.

Just then—
    amid tittering and whispers—
my tow-headed trio appears.

Amy walks on tiptoe,
    carries bubbling 7-Up
        in her favorite cup.

Nathan grins behind a card
    with cut-out animals;
        "G∃T W∃LL" is printed
        in bold red crayon.

Brett bears a freshly picked bouquet—
    Queen Anne's lace and sweet clover
        in an old glass jar.

I shuffle stuff
        from the cluttered table
    to make room for the
        best medicine of all—

a Bozo cup
    a paste-smeared card
        a very special mayonnaise jar.

24

Here I am on my hands and knees,
  cleaning the living room rug.
Fuzzy puffs of white
    melt beneath my scrub brush;
  fumes burn my nose.
I push damp hair off my forehead
  and sigh.

A perfect Monday morning chore.

Last Friday I prepared the room
  for this final act of
    purification—
swept down walls and corners,
destroyed concealed webs while
  wispy spiders scrambled for safety.

Now I glance toward baseboards
  and see in disgust
    almost all the webs have reappeared!
And I realize my error:
  I eliminated webs
    but left spiders.

On soggy knees I contemplate
  how often in my own life
    I brush only the surface—
      attempt changes
    while failing to
      abolish causes.

I rise to arm myself with
  insecticide and broom,
and pray a silent prayer
  to be rid of spiders
    as well as webs.

Fireflies flicker in the outfield
  as this Little League game begins.

Matching baseball jerseys—
  freshly Clorox-white
  first-inning clean—
proclaim the names of sponsors:
    OTTO REALTY
    LEMON'S FLORIST

Awkward mitts hang heavy
  on the hands of bantam basemen.
Behind home plate crouches the catcher,
  weighted with safety equipment
  looking like a muzzled bumblebee.

Bent knees push against
  patched blue jeans
as the lead-off batter waits
  for that perfect pitch.

Chatter drifts through
  popcorn-scented dusk.

the pitch—
  the hit—

And suddenly bleachers reel
  with the squeals of excited parents.

Small gray clouds rise from dirty tennies
  as the slugger rounds bases.
Home plate blurs
  beneath a cloud of dust.

He slides—
  the season's first home run!

Teams take turns at bat,
  filling innings with
pop-ups and strikeouts
  line drives and overthrows.

Heroes are born
  with each crack of the bat.
Heartache hovers close
  as a fumbled fly.

Armed with postgame Cokes,
  coach gathers his
    dirt-covered brood
    into the dugout

where each boy gets
  a cold drink
    a bit of seasoned advice
      a quick, hard hug.

Soon players emerge
  jostling and bragging
  predicting the best season ever
    radiant with the reality of
      coach's tough,
      unconditional
        love.

Teach me, Lord
  to trust your constancy.
Let me learn
  to expect the hugs.

And give me, God
  the faith to feel loved—
even when I
  strike out.

26

This morning I drive through mountains
   half a millennium old.
The highway winds upward
   in long, dark arcs—
its asphalt silhouette
   looking like the bodies of black snakes
   I used to catch in September cornfields.

Pine trees grow in profusion,
   peaks stretching toward the
   distant blue of hazy skies.
At the base of the mountains,
   daisies bloom—
their lithe bodies
   swaying in the swoosh of
   watermelon-laden semis.

As I drink in passing scenery
   peace settles on me,
assuring me that
   God indeed cares about
   even the littlest
     things in my life—

for he who sculpted the
   mighty mountains

took time to create the
   daisies, too.

Autumn

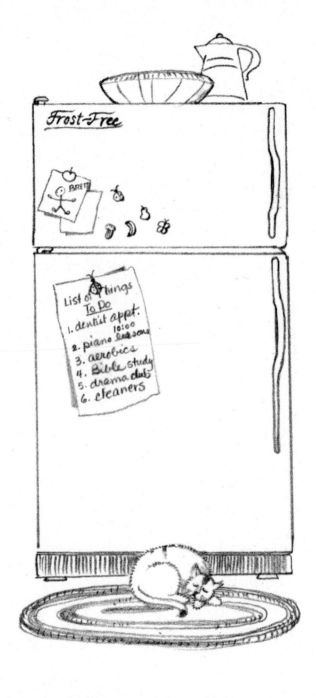

27

It's Monday morning
  and yet,
miraculously enough,

    no one overslept
              missed the bus
                  forgot his lunch money
    no one spilled orange juice
              stepped on the dog's tail
                  or even slammed the door.

On the refrigerator
  hangs this week's calendar,
its fat white squares
  filled with jottings:

              dentist appointment
              piano lesson
                aerobics
              Bible study
              drama club
                cleaners
              allergy shots
              racquetball . . .

But for now,
  with September sun
  shining through my
  starched priscillas,

I pour a second cup of coffee
  watch sun rays play near freshly cut mums
and
  lift my cup
    in a mute salute
    to this Monday morning
so well-begun.

28

My life is made
 of mismatched socks
that mysteriously emerge
 from baskets of
  freshly dried clothes.

I place them aside,
 supposing a partner will appear.
But soon unmated colors
 lie in piles
  like limp confetti.

Yet I keep them,
 these mismatched socks,
and sometimes—
 when I move the dresser
  or clean out drawers
   or fish behind the dryer

a mate magically appears

 to remind me of
  the importance of
   hope.

29

Oh God,
my son starts school today.

Stiff-soled new shoes
   make faint squeaks
as he crosses the kitchen linoleum.

He gulps his cereal,
   slurping the milk
      from his spoon.

I glance out the front window.

Sheet after sheet of gray rain
   descends in slanted assaults.

I had hoped for sunshine.

He stands before me
   in his yellow rain slicker,
elfin in its pointed hood
          too-long sleeves.

His eyes show a strange mixture of
   anticipation and fear
      longing and regret.

There's so much I want to say—
but the lump in my throat
   grows larger
and I only manage a mumbled
   "I love you."

He hugs me;
I kiss his sunburned cheek.

He walks alone to the bus stop,
  avoiding murky puddles—
a sign of new maturity
          of schoolday dignity.

Amid blinking lights,
  he boards the bus.
It waddles down the road
  away from tricycles
            "Sesame Street"
      and me.

Be with him, Lord.

The world is so big,
  and he is so very small.

Hover close as he
  tries his wings.
Pick him up after those
  predictable
    inevitable
falls.

But Father—
don't let him
  fly too far
      too soon.

He's still my baby,
  after all.

30

My "knight in shining armor"
  drives a red pickup
  wears flannel shirts
    and flaunts a ragged baseball cap
      instead of a plume.

He brings me lilac bouquets,
  not long-stem roses.
Sonnets aren't his style,
  but he has the most eloquent eyes.

And I'm his "damsel in distress"
  whenever the kitchen sink clogs
            my car won't start
            the baby has colic—again.

He romps with our kids
  picks up his dirty socks
  holds me when I'm blue
    and still calls me "Honey."

He lets me cry at movies
            befriend stray cats
              sleep in on Saturday mornings.

He fights fierce dragons—
  INFLATION, UNEMPLOYMENT—
and emerges with the spring
  still in his step.

He is my lover
        my provider
        my husband—

who helps me through
  Mondays and
    other traumas.

31

Tiny teacups
  filled with water.
Cracker squares
  on plastic plates.

"Can I get you more tea, Mommy?"

My daughter makes the perfect hostess,
  her high heels clomping
    as she refills my cup
  her floppy hat half hiding
    rouge-red cheeks.

We talk about
  birthday parties
  what animal we'd like to be
  suppose you had three wishes . . .
  how totally gross earthworms feel.

"Have another cracker."
  She pushes the plate toward me.
"They're really quite good today."

I nibble on its salty edges
  while my daughter attends
to other guests:
  a lumpy teddy bear
    with frayed purple bow
  a giant Raggedy Ann
    with eyes the color of coal.

Happiness
  dances behind her dimples

as she fluffs and pushes
    her stuffed friends into place,
making sure each guest is
    comfy
        well-fed
            happy.

When did I lose it, Lord—
    the joy of serving others
    the contentment of commitment.

Humble me that I may see
    true greatness comes
        not in being served
        but in serving.

Remind me that on bended knee
    you washed the disciples' feet—
you, who set planets spinning
    you, who spoke beasts into being.

Teach me to seek the
    simplicity of service.

Let me feel again that perfect joy
    my daughter knows in
serving tea to
    teddy bears
        rag dolls
            and me.

32

Oak chairs with slat backs
    like jail bars
line the fat Formica table—
    covered with square glass ashtrays
                    packages of crackers
                        teaspoons crusty with
                            dried coffee.

The bailiff swoops in with
    Styrofoam cups and
        fingerprinted coffee urn.
She bubbles like
    a social director
        on a cruise ship.
"Coffee will be done about the time
    they call you in. Ha. Ha. Ha.
Hang your coats in the closet."

Stumbling over boxes,
    I reach for a wrinkled hanger
        dangling against the far wall

then sit on the edge of my chair,
    listening for my name
        as she reads aloud
THE JURY LIST.

My name is called.

I manage a muttered
    "Here."

And this Monday becomes
    forever fixed in my memory

for today I must
    sit in the seat of judgment
        weigh the evidence
            determine innocence
or guilt.

I must confine myself to facts—
    mercy is not a matter for
        THE JURY.

Much later,
I sit staring out my windshield
    past the steel-gray head
        of my expired parking meter
    to the slate-gray courthouse,
        huge and ominous in the fading light.

My head aches with
    the echoes of "Guilty"
        the resounding rap of the gavel.

As I pull into rush-hour traffic,
    tears tumble down my cheeks—

tears of frustration for
    wasted lives
tears of anger at
    inevitable
        consequences

and tears of gratitude
    that in my case
mercy—not justice—
    was God's chosen option.

33

Today was my turn
  to carpool the kids.

It was after I turned off the highway
                headed for home
that I passed her—
  stern-faced
    sweat-soaked
        body bobbing in steady rhythm
            while feet pounded the pavement.

I watched in my rearview mirror
  till her blue sweat suit
    was only a blob in the distance,

and how I envied
  her dedication!

Last week we saw a family biking.

I promptly determined
  to dust off the cobwebs
    air up the tires
      resurrect my old Schwinn
for a Saturday outing.

But my bike's still in the garage—
  buried beneath half-filled paint cans
                rusting lawn furniture.

What's wrong with me, God?

I feel trapped
  in a circle
    of futile intent

personally
  spiritually

I feel the frustration
  of unfulfilled goals
    fruitless resolutions.

Help me on this Monday
  to begin my new week
with a new wave of
  self-discipline,
  realism.

Let me not be content
  to imitate others.

But initiate in
  me
what best will serve
  you.

34

I've changed clothes
   three times this morning,

searching for the right outfit—
   understated
      but not plain
   sophisticated
      but not stuffy . . .

because on this Monday morning
   at 10:15 sharp
I have a conference
   with my son's teacher.

It seems he's neglecting his work.
   Again.
It seems he's a discipline problem.
   Again.
It seems he can't interact well.
   Again.

I feel so disappointed, God—
   in him
      in me.

I've tried
   authority/
      leniency
   bullying/
      bargaining.

I've tried
   tears and
      tantrums and
         prayer—

but this morning
    I face my son's teacher
with no pat answers
    no foolproof plan.

Give me wisdom, Father
    to cope with my anger
    to profit from past mistakes
        to keep communicating

and let me take comfort
    in the reality that
the good Lord himself
    has trouble with his children, too.

35

I took my three-year-old
  bike riding this morning.
As I pedaled along country roads
  trees and foliage
  fairly screamed with color—
    bronze, scarlet, tangerine.

That maple-lined hill hadn't looked so large.
But halfway up I found myself
  huffing and puffing,
  forced to stand up and
    PUSH, PUSH, PUSH those pedals.
At the top I paused for breath—
  feeling the blood in my cheeks
        the aching in my calves.

My son—whose infant seat
  assured him a worry-free ride—
  giggled, "Boy, my legs are tired."

His legs indeed!

Then I thought suddenly of
  that problem that troubled my sleep
  the burden that weighted my heart
and I realized
  God carries both me and my cares
    if only I trust and rest in him.

I turned the bike,
  began coasting downhill,
frosty air blowing my hair
  slants of autumn sun patterning my pathway
and I suddenly felt
  very
    very
      light.

36

Peanut butter kisses
  wrapped in black and orange
cellophane squares filled
  with candy corn
plastic pumpkins empty
  except for candy wrappers.

These are the
  "Trick-or-Treat" memoirs
that clutter my house
  this post-Halloween Monday.

My six-year-old comes
  downstairs for breakfast.

She wears her fairy princess costume—
  complete with cardboard-star wand
                    tinfoil crown
                      dime-store mask.

I pretend not to notice,
  suppress a laugh
    as she attempts
    to shove her cornflakes
      through the smiling slit.

But as the mask comes off
  I see the tears—
    glistening like glass beads,
    threatening an avalanche.

"What's wrong, Honey?
  Why the costume?
Halloween's over you know . . ."

The avalanche begins.

"Mommy, I like *this* me.

I don't like the other me—
   not at all!"
I hold the fairy princess close;
   her chiffon layers shake
     with the force of her sobs.

"I love you, Honey.
   And so does God.
     Just the way you are."

We talk
   and pray
     and finally

she scurries for the bus,
   her red jogging suit
   flitting like a cardinal
     down the drive.

As I pick up the mask,
   I finger its rigid features.

And my heart is pricked
   to realize
     how often
I, too, hide—

frightened to show the real me
   fearing the flawed image
     feigning self-sufficiency.

So on this frosty Monday, God—
   as I pack up
     paper pumpkins
     crinkled costumes—

give me the strength
   to put away
     my own masks as well

give me the courage

to accept from you
   a graciously given treat—

the unabashed freedom
   to be me.

37

How did all the leaves
   know to fall today—

the first Monday
   of November?

In one crusty night of
   forty-degree rain
the brittle beauty of
   October is gone.

Branches stretch empty hands
   toward skies that
      darken too early.

I drag my rusty rake
   through piles of leaves
mound them into mountains
   of soggy brown.

A gray squirrel chatters down at me
   from a nearby tree.
He runs round and round the trunk,
   like the endlessly moving
      stripes on a barber's pole.

Then,
with a flamboyant flash
   of his furry tail,
friend squirrel scurries off
   to scavenge for winter nuts—

leaving me leaning
   on the handle of my rake
      determining the things I should
         "store up" for coming months:

the warmth of August afternoons
    a little July sunshine
the gentleness of full-moon October nights

    and the optimism
        of a March crocus.

38

Monday morning mending
　　lies on the laundry room floor.

Piled knee-high are
　　torn jeans
　　　　ripped sleeves
　　　　　　buttonless blouses.

My son's jeans
　　show shredded knees;
frayed threads dangle
　　across the expanse
　　　　like fragile rope bridges.

The sleeve of
　　my daughter's red dress
　　　　sags;
a gaping hole
　　stares up at me.

Two—
　　no, three—
buttons are missing
　　from my ruffled white blouse.

Admittedly I remember
　　a certain shiny worn spot
　　　　stray red threads
　　　　　　several loose buttons.

But all were simply
　　small problems
　　　　I'd get to
soon . . .

and now my arms
    are loaded down with
        battered
            tattered
                togs.

I watch my silver needle
        slither through polyester
    wonder what other
        small problems
            need my attention
now . . .

    a hasty word
    some misplaced blame
    that grudge grown large
        with longevity.

Help me on this Monday, Lord
    lest—
lost in patches and spools of thread—
    I forget now to mend
        the freshly frayed fringes
            of my own life.

39

Last week was spent
   poring over my yearbook,
   quizzing myself on names of
     high school classmates.

Forgotten faces stare at me
   from pages framed with autographs.
Teachers with tired eyes
   pose behind cluttered desks.

All week long
   I kept that yearbook close,
using every spare moment
   to memorize the names of
never-to-be-forgotten friends.

Then Saturday night was our class reunion . . .

Crepe paper swags of blue and gold
   sag across doorways.

Females cluster in corners,
   their matronly figures belying the fact
they were once high-stepping majorettes
                varsity cheerleaders.

Athletes with sagging stomachs
   slap one another on the back,
tell again how they made that
   final point in '65.

We show pictures of our children
   name-drop tropical seaports where last
     we vacationed

mention the make and model of cars
   we drive
complain about how much income tax
   we paid last year

and comment—
   over and over and over
how none of us has changed,
   how none of us looks a day older.

We say it often and loudly
   because we all know
      it isn't true.

Jimmy Bowman
   who walked me to the restaurant every noon
   and let me wear his letter jacket
      once
is bald.

Janie
   my best-forever friend
   whose wedding we planned over
      Hostess cupcakes and cherry Cokes
could think of little to say to me now.

Kenny Limburg
   who threw me third-grade kisses
   through school bus windows
didn't even recognize me.

But there were other changes, too.

Sharon's traded her pompons
   for a briefcase
   and a promising place
      in a large law firm.

Rocky "knock-'em-dead" Piganelli
    is now a priest
    in New York's inner city.

Homely Harriet married a doctor
    and has three children—
    three *beautiful* children.

As we part,
    we hug and promise to write,
each making mental commitments
    at least to exchange
        Christmas cards.

Driving home,
I glance at myself in the rearview mirror,
    realizing how little I resemble
that wide-eyed senior
    smiling forever between the
        covers of my high school yearbook.

But suddenly I don't care.

After all—
    change is the essence of life:
        buds bloom into roses
        saplings become pines
        tadpoles turn to frogs
cocoons give way to butterflies

and I can hardly wait to see
    what I'll turn out to be
tomorrow . . .

Winter

40

This morning a missionary
   spoke to our women's ministries.

Her hair was curly and thick,
   pulled back with a fat, brown barrette.
As she spoke, tiny tendrils fell forward
   to frame her tanned face.

Her eyes were the gray of Lake Michigan waves,
   and held you with an intensity
seldom seen among Midwest housewives.

She spoke of mountain sunsets and hepatitis
         abandoned babies and beggar boys
         dirt-floor churches and wild orchids.

The hum of her projector
   vibrated the darkness
as colorful slides slid by on the wall—
   their backgrounds looking like
      Caribbean travel brochures.

Dark-skinned people stared out at me,
   their bare feet firmly planted on mountain paths
   their posture perfect and fluid as they balance
      huge baskets of fruit on their heads.

Click after click
   the parade continued—

a small boy
   bent with the weight of
   his wooden-wheel cart,
      where a freshly killed pig
      leaves a spattered trail of blood

a crippled beggar
   crumpled on a street corner,
      holding a battered cup
      with his two-fingered hand

a chapel cross
   dark and small against
      an apricot sky.

I blink back tears
   and wonder why I am really crying—

because the need is so great
   or my world so small.

Help me God,
   for suburbia seems
      a mundane mission field.

Remind me that unbelievers
   come in all colors and costumes.

Bless our efforts, Lord
   and let us all be fruitful—

whether the fruit we harvest
   is the exotic
      or domestic kind.

41

The season's first snowflakes
  flirt with my wipers.
December.
  Already.

"Impossible!"
  I say aloud
to a passing semi piled high
  with a load of Christmas trees,
    their scented boughs
    bound with brown twine.

The mall now boasts
  a festive look—
white lights wink
  through wisps of
    plastic greenery
poinsettias pose
  behind plate glass
giant candy canes
  stand sentry
    inside display windows.

The twang of
  worn Christmas records
    ripples from square black speakers.

Santa sits in a
  scarlet sleigh;
his eyes look tired.
A petite blond in
  skimpy red velvet
    snaps picture
        after
          picture.

I haven't begun
   to think yet of
      Christmas, God.

My refrigerator
is still filled with
   leftover turkey
   dried-out dressing.

Yet Christmas is here,
   its presence as tangible as
      cardboard snowflakes
         suspended on silver threads
         high above my head.

Help me this year, Lord
   to sidestep the surge of
      commercialism
      materialism
that swirls around me
   in colorful waves.

Above the BRRINGG of cash registers
                  the ripping of Christmas wrap
let me hear the
   rustle of swaddling cloth
      cradled in straw.

In the midst of
   bow-making
      cookie-baking
let me take time for
   the most important
      preparation
of all—

   the opening of
   my own heart
      to you.

42

I have always been a
  fudge failure,
condemned to pans of syrupy black
            to plates of brick-hard squares.

But this new recipe
  is for the
    "NEVER-FAIL" kind—
and I plunge in with
  determined optimism.

Yet halfway through the process
  things look bleak;
a wad of dark mixture
  clings to my spoon.

I reread directions,
then forge ahead
  with blind trust in the
  unseen creator of this
    NEVER-FAIL FUDGE.

Later,
  as I admire cooling platters
    of creamy, flawless fudge

I ponder the wonder
  of trust—

and open my Bible
to read again
  God's
    never-fail
        directions
for my life.

43

Today is the Christmas assembly.

I sit with other parents
    on brown metal chairs,
all watching the orchestra
        file into the gym
    wondering when our children
        became so tall
                so grown-up
                so serious.

Florescent lights glint off
    brightly polished baritones
    highly buffed cellos.

Stuffy air is shattered by
    scrambled sounds of squeals and plinks
    rumbling groans of bows
        drawn across taut strings
as each musician
    tackles the task of tuning.

The conductor steps onto
    the small black platform,
        flanked by poinsettias and pine.

Silence.

His baton hovers in the air
    like a mute hummingbird.

Every eye is his.

The baton moves lightly;
    the music begins—

filling the gym with
   stirring strains of remembered carols
   melodic magic of well-orchestrated parts

and I silently celebrate
   the birth of Christ
who
   tunes
     orchestrates
      conducts
my life.

44

With a deftness born of repetition,
　I butter and jelly my son's toast.

He sits in front of the T.V.,
　lost in a cartoon world of
　　talking cats
　　amazing mice.

I cut his toast in half,
　call him to the breakfast table.
His tiny hand struggles
　to hold the half-slice.
Jelly oozes onto his thumb.

"Would you like me to cut your toast again?
　Then you will have four pieces."

He studies his plate for a moment.
　Then, wide-eyed and serious, says
"Oh, Mommy—I could never eat
　　four pieces of toast!
But I can eat just these *two*."

I rumple his tousled curls
　and smile.

"It's all a matter of perspective,"
　I think to myself
as I squirt detergent into
　bubbling water.

But as I do dishes,
　the wisdom of his words
　　unwinds in my mind.

How often do I
    achieve
or
    fail
based simply on
    how something
        seems to be
to me?

How much success
    do I fail to possess
because of faulty ambition
                    faithless vision?

Give me, God
    the courage to be clearsighted
        the confidence to accomplish.

I watch as my son
    stuffs the last crust into his mouth
    methodically licks jelly from his fingers;

then I pray a prayer of thanks
    for this continuing Truth:
"A little child shall lead them."

45

The first Monday
  of this new year
    stands before me—

pregnant with possibilities
  dressed in New Year's resolutions.

I leaf through
  my new calendar;
    Halloween
      Flag Day
        Advent
flip by in a blur
  of dark numbers
    blank squares.

A new day.
  A new week.
    A new year . . .

but the same old me, God—
  with my flaws
    my problems
      my probability for error.

So on this virgin Monday, Lord
  grant me the courage
    to try anew.

And make my heart
  as clean
    as available
      as uncluttered
as these small white squares
  of my new year's calendar.

46

My son's tennis shoes
   sit drying in my kitchen window,
their frayed laces
   dangling across worn toes
                    torn seams.

He needs new shoes.
   Again.

My daughter's braces go on next week,
   at a figure that made my hand shake
   as I wrote out the initial payment.

The dog needs shots.

My washer is making
   grating, threatening noises
that hint of
   imminent and permanent disability.

Utility bills rise
   like hot air balloons;
for both it seems the
   sky's the limit.

Our nest egg is just a
   scrambled stack of
      withdrawals and
      second notices.

"The love of money is the root of all evil."

I was raised on that verse—
   that and oatmeal-filled meatloaf . . .

so I'm not asking to be rich, Lord,
   but would solvency be such a sin?

And, as if bills aren't enough,
   daily I am bombarded by
   needy, worthwhile causes:

   that letter from the Arizona reservation
my neighbor who hasn't worked in months
a call about the community food pantry
   the lady from the March of Dimes
   my local church's building fund.

Help me, Father
   to economize
      prioritize.

Keep me from equating
   money with happiness
      affluence with success.

Teach me to live simply
         to give wisely yet freely
   of my frugal means

remembering that sometimes
   money—
      like loaves and fishes—
multiplies when shared.

47

This wintery Monday
  finds us wrapped in a crystal cocoon.
No school buses brave the blizzard.
No snowplows throw back
  this blanket of white.

Outside
  wind moans around corners,
    rattling startled window panes
  snow blows in frenzied whirlwinds,
    wrapping fenceposts in frosty angel hair.

Inside
  a strange quiet hovers;
    children cower or
          pout or
            silently seethe
since I—
  in a burst of temper—
exiled them to their rooms.

I didn't mean it to be this way, God.

Snowdays are for
  popping corn
    baking cookies
      playing endless games of Monopoly.

But their exuberance
  grew too rude
    their excitement
      too rowdy

and I heard myself
   scolding
      screaming
evicting.

But now,
   as I sit at the kitchen table,
      frustrated
         embarrassed
ashamed

I hear the
   ting-lang
   cling-clang
      of my wind chime's uneven jingling
rising above the storm
      like a hymn.

And I realize the
   needlessness of clamor
      necessity of control.

So on this snowbound Monday, Lord
   remind me that
      life's most important words
         are often whispered—

words like "I love you."
   words like "I'm sorry."

48

Brooms swish
  against dark linoleum,
swiping at brunette swirls
      blonde curls.

Fake fig trees
  frame rows of
ragged rattan hampers,
  holding towels with
    frayed edges.

Water sprays from a snaky hose,
  splashes against my hair.
With practiced nonchalance
  the shampoo girl
    massages my scalp.
Her gum cracks and pops
  with each push of her painted nails.

This has been a
  month of Mondays
    spent at the beauty shop.

It seems my permanent waves
  are less than permanent.

So for the third time in four weeks,
  permanent papers
close around my damp hair,
  wound on rollers the
    color of cotton candy.

Coils of cotton
  frame my face,
holding back the smelly solution.

To pass time under the
   bubble-domed dryer
I try listing the
   "permanent" things in my life:
      home, husband
      children, church

only to realize
   how terribly temporal
      these things can be.

I try again.

"Lo, I am with you always."
The words seem whispered
   in the whoosh of warm air.

Later,
as I drive home,

I wonder how long these
   curls will last—
how fleeting will be the flip
   they grant my frosted hair.

"Lo, I am with you always."

I say the words aloud,
   toss my fresh ringlets,

and smile with the assurance that
   amid life's insecurities
God's presence makes
   abundant
      permanence.

49

Winds rattle cold window glass,
   twirling shafts of snow
tossing crumpled oak leaves skyward.

I peek through panes etched with frost,
   past corner swirls of crystal.

My mailbox is hardly visible.

It sits like a gray hump
   atop a snow mountain,
its red flag a remnant feather
   of a picaresque cardinal.

Bundled in layers of flannel and wool,
   I trudge down the driveway—
my fur-lined boots
   leaving crinkled imprints
     in the snow's icy crust.

I pull open the
   metal mouth of my mailbox.
Feather-light snowflakes
   tumble inside,
landing on the colorful cover
   of a spring seed catalogue.

With mittened clumsiness
   I turn its snow-spattered pages:

crimson maples, pink plums
   blossoming crab apples
     scarlet strawberries
endless rows of Shasta daisies.

Then suddenly,
   through eyelashes laden with snow lace,
I see my yard
   shimmer in shades of summer green.
Rainbow-colored flowers
   grow in profusion,
      bordering each walk
         brightening each doorway.

Back inside,
   I look again toward
my cold, white yard—

to understand anew
      that faith really is
the substance of things hoped for
   the evidence of things not seen.

And thinking of spring
   I smile a chapped-cheek smile,
as I shake snow—
   and the scent of azaleas—
from my mittens.

50

Brown lunch sacks
   stand at attention,
      their bottoms weighted
      with rosy red apples.

I deftly apply
   peanut butter and jelly
      to slices of bread
      sprawled on my kitchen counter.

I've packed so many lunches, God.

Sometimes it seems my past
   is one long line of
      brown bags
      bologna sandwiches
      saran-wrapped cookies

and yet

this simple task
   unites me with
      other women—
everywhere and always:

with the miner's wife
   who packs a pouch
      of biscuits and cold bacon

with the brand new bride
   who tucks inside
      lumpy homemade brownies

with the mother of a long-ago lad
   who tenderly wrapped
      five loaves and two small fishes.

Bless these humble efforts, Lord
   as once you blessed those
      loaves and fishes.

Multiply the love
   packed in brown lunch sacks—
everywhere and always.

51

The fragrance of flowers
   fills the room
with a shroud-like closeness.

Aunt Rinda
   lies in a casket
      lined with gray silk
her silver curls
   cascading onto the pillow.

Her eyes are closed—
   and for a minute
I remember childhood games of
   hide-and-seek
with Aunt Rinda's clear voice
   echoing through barnyard twilight,
      "ninety-six, ninety-seven . . ."
while we scurried to hide in
   corn bins or hay mows or bean fields.

Even now her pink lips
   seem puckered in a playful
      "one hundred!"

But as I watch and wait,
   the reality of death
seeps into my pores
   like February fog.

Gently I touch my stomach,
   its firm round mound
obvious in my black crepe dress.

It seems ludicrous, somehow
   to be pregnant at a funeral—

to flaunt the imminence of new life
  in the face of death.

Organ music spills
  from black speakers;
mourners file past
  like sheep.

When suddenly
  my baby moves—
a strong, hard kick
  that ripples out in quivers—

as if to tell me
  that life unseen
    is no less life
  that miracles unfathomed
    are no less miracles.

I touch the fronds
  of a nearby fern,
taking new comfort in
  Life
    around me
    within me
      beyond me.

52

My Monday morning alarm blares
    in the darkness of my bedroom.
I fumble with its clanking body,
    finally silence its clamor.

"Five more minutes . . ."
    I mumble to myself.
Snuggling into my blankets,
    I drift toward the warmth of sleep

when suddenly—
    like a punch in the stomach—
I remember the cause
    for my early alarm:

my admitted need
    for a "quiet time"
before breakfast bedlam
            school bus scurry
                today's first sibling spat.

Grudgingly,
I throw back covers
    slip my feet into furry slippers
        grab my Bible
and head for the kitchen.

Through half-opened eyes
    I skim the first chapter
        of Saint Mark,
mechanically reading
    word after word
        verse after verse—

but something in verse 35
    demands my attention.
I reread—

"And in the morning,
    rising up a great while before day,
Jesus . . . departed to a solitary place,
    and there prayed."

I glance around my kitchen:
    coffee pot poised for perking
    toaster waiting with open mouth
        for slices of raisin bread
    lunch boxes lined up like
        colorful building blocks.

Help me, Father
    to come in early morning quietness
        to this, my "solitary place."

Let me achieve the
    discipline and devotion
        to slough off the comforts of sleep

for I would be like you,
    my Lord—

not only
    in the heat of the day
but also
    in the way
you found an early morning
    place to pray.